GW01367658

GREAT ADVENTURE

Learning new survival skills will make any walk in the woods or through fields much more enjoyable. To be able to identify a plant and know its uses is a wonderful thing and you will develop a much better relationship with the natural world.

This book is a first step for you to learn about survival. A good knowledge of survival techniques can, and has, saved lives in the past. Who knows, perhaps one day it might save yours!

WARNING!

Never go out without an adult. Practise these skills in your garden.

PREPARATION

The most important thing you can do to ensure your survival is to BE PREPARED.

PERFECT PLANNING

The best way to survive is to use your brain. Humans have been around for thousands of years and we've survived because we've used our intelligence. If you don't plan your trip properly you may be at a loss as to what to do if something goes wrong.

BASIC SURVIVAL SKILLS

Written by Mike Jarmain
Illustrated by Peter Wilks and Geoff Ball

TOP THAT! Kids™

Published by Top That! Publishing plc
Tide Mill Way, Woodbridge, Suffolk, IP12 1AP, UK
www.topthatpublishing.com
Copyright © 2005 Top That! Publishing plc
Top That! Kids is a trademark of Top That! Publishing plc
Mini Maestro is a Registered Trademark of Top That! Publishing plc
All rights reserved

SURVIVAL SKILLS

As long as people enjoy activities in the great outdoors, there will be a need to know about survival. This is the skill of using what nature provides to keep you alive.

AMAZING NATURE

Survival is about learning to understand and respect nature. It is incredible what people can eat, make or use from the natural resources around them.

'MUST GO' EQUIPMENT

When we go out into any wild areas there are some things that we absolutely must take with us. These are called 'must go items'. They include such things as a torch, a compass, food, some warm clothing and a waterproof jacket and trousers.

TRIP PLAN

It is essential that you leave details behind of where you are going, how long you will be away, what kit you have with you, etc. If anything happens, the trip plan is the best way for the emergency services to find and help you. Always fill it in before visiting any wilderness area and leave a copy with a responsible person.

COLLECTING WATER

Water is likely to be your number one priority in any survival situation. Make sure you always take plenty of water on a trip

Sweating, eating, even breathing, all takes water from your body and you need to replace it. Some of the easiest ways to collect it are:

1 Rain. Use anything you have to collect the rainwater. You should be able to drink rainwater without purifying it but, if unsure, purify.

2 Soaking up the dew. You need to get up before dawn and use a shirt as a sponge to mop up the dew before the sun evaporates it. Wring the water out into a container and then purify. Hey presto, drinking water!

3 Streams and rivers. Water always runs downhill so the best place to look for streams and rivers is in valley bottoms.

There are other methods of acquiring water but these methods are very easy and straightforward. If you can master all of them, you should never go short of water.

PURIFYING WATER

Generally, the only water which can be safely drunk is rainwater. All other water will have to be purified to make it safe to drink.

DISEASES

If you don't do this, you may suffer from the numerous water-borne diseases. These include bilharzia, polio, cholera, hookworm, amoebic dysentery and leptospirosis. They are as bad for you as they are difficult to spell!

METHODS

1. **Chlorine-based purification tablets (puritabs)** – these are small tablets which make water safe to drink but leave it with a taste a little like swimming pool water.

2 Iodine-based purification tablets – these are very similar in size to the chlorine puritabs apart from iodine being the chemical used to make the water safe.

3 Commercial filtration kits – these kits, which are becoming increasingly common, filter the water and purify it at the same time. Not all purification kits leave water 100% safe to drink and the filter will have to be changed fairly regularly.

WILDERNESS FISHING

Fish are a readily available source of food in many areas of the world.

WHERE TO FISH

In hot weather, fish tend to gather in deeper, cooler water. Look for shady pools in rivers and streams. In cold weather, fish tend to move to shallower, slightly warmer water. Experience will make you more aware of where to look for fish.

WHEN TO FISH

Some of the best times to fish are just before dawn or just after dusk. Other good times include before a storm (fishing is usually poor during and after one), at night when the moon is full and when there is a lot of fish movement at the surface.

BOTTLE TRAPS

A good way of catching small fish is to make a bottle trap. Cut the top one-third off a plastic bottle, invert it and place inside the remaining two-thirds. Put some bait inside and place on the bottom of a stream. Most fish that swim in will be unable to swim out.

NETS

If you have a net or can make one, you will find fishing a very simple process. Nets do not weigh very much but are deadly efficient. In fact, if you use one in a river, you will have to be careful that you do not take all the fish near you.

WARNING!
Never go near rivers without an adult.

WHERE TO SHELTER

One of the most important things in survival is to learn how to erect an effective shelter, whether from natural or man-made materials.

LOCATION

If you have to make a shelter, it is very important that you allow yourself enough time to put it up in daylight. Look for a safe location, sheltered from the wind, rain, sun and away from any danger of rockslides or suspect tree branches.

FLOODING

You want to be reasonably close to a water supply but do not build your shelter in a ditch or any kind of water runoff! Flooding could well result in you being in your water supply, leading to loss of all your equipment or worse.

ANIMALS

Stay away from any animal trails, especially around any watering areas. Animals will trample straight through your shelter and definitely ruin your sleep.

TYPES OF SHELTER

Shelter is necessary to give shade, repel wind and rain and to keep in warmth.

KENNEL

A long ridge pole is held up at about waist height and sticks are leant against it. The whole thing is then covered with a deep layer of leaf litter to make it wind and waterproof. Some branches are then laid on top to hold everything in place.

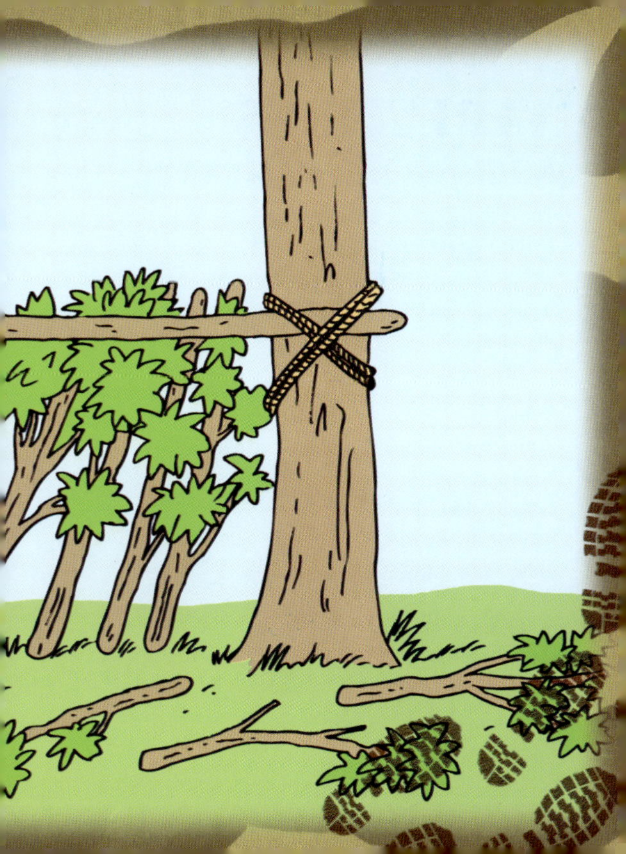

VARIATIONS
SHELTER SHEET KENNEL

The ridge pole is placed in position and then your shelter sheet placed over the top. Both sides are secured so they lie at a steep angle. Much quicker to put up than using sticks and leaf litter but not as warm.

LEAN TO

The classic survival shelter. Once constructed, it will last for a very long time. Windproof, waterproof, warm and sturdy when built properly. Much quicker to build if several people take part.

FALLEN TRUNK

Make use of any branches which sweep down to the ground or boughs which have partly broken from the tree to give basic shelter from the elements – but make sure that they're not so broken that they might fall on you.

BEDDING

Do not lie on the bare ground. It will drain all the heat out of you. Small springy branches are excellent for making a 'mat' to lie on top of. Failing that, use anything to insulate you from the ground.

NATURAL CORD AND BINDINGS

From tying your shoelaces to making a climbing rope, nature provides all the raw materials we need.

WHAT TO LOOK FOR

There are three things that any potential source of cord must have – length, strength and flexibility. Without these three qualities, any cord you make will probably not be very strong. Making it carefully and using robust materials will result in a strong rope.

MAKING ROPE

Rope and cord can be made from a huge variety of things. The list of plants that we can use includes stinging nettles, thistles, vines, rushes and long grass. Rope can also be made from tree bark, some plant leaves, palms and coconut husks.

DID YOU KNOW?

The Aztecs used to make bridges across very deep canyons out of grass! You can also use thin roots from trees, hair and sinew (tendons) from dead animals. Sinew makes the strongest cord and was traditionally used for bow strings.

MAKING NETTLE CORD

Nettle cord makes one of the strongest natural cords. It is quite easy to make and people have even made fishing nets out of it.

STEP 1

Collect the longest nettles you can find. Wear gloves to ensure you don't get stung. Cut the nettle at its base – DO NOT pull it up with its roots. Cut it and it will re-grow next year. Pull up the roots and it will die.

STEP 2

Strip all the leaves off the stem by running your hand from the base towards the top. Don't do it the other way around, as you may remove material which you need for making the cord.

STEP 3

Lay the stem on a hard surface and gently pound it with a smooth stone. Use your thumbnail to open up the stem and lay it flat.

STEP 4

Estimate a point one-third up the stem and carefully fold the stem so the core breaks. You can now strip the outer material away from the core. Discard the inner core and hang the outer material to dry. It will soon be ready to be spun into cord.

SPINNING THE FIBRES INTO CORD

Once the fibres are dry, they are ready to be spun into cord.

STEP 1

Pick up one of the strands. Hold it in your hand so that two-thirds hang to the right (A), and one-third to the left (B).

STEP 2

Holding B in you left hand, dampen the index finger and thumb of your right hand and roll the fibre between your fingers in clockwise direction. Moving from left to right, twist the whole fibre into a strand.

STEP 3

Then, to secure the twist, take the middle in your teeth and bring the two ends together. When you let go the strand will twist around itself naturally. Repeat steps 1 and 2 with another fibre. Then take the two twisted strands (A and B) and wrap them around one another, as shown.

STEP 4

When knotted on the end to keep it from unreeling, the result will be strong cordage.

KNOTS

By learning how to correctly tie a few knots, you will make any time in the wilderness a more enjoyable but ultimately much safer experience.

BOWLINE

This is a very easily tied loop that has many uses. It will not tighten or come undone when loaded with weight and so can be used as a lifeline.

CLOVE HITCH

This is one of the most commonly tied knots. It can be used for tying things to a post or bar.

REEF KNOT

One of the first knots people learn to tie. Useful for tying something securely but also easy to undo. Don't tie it with nylon cord or to join different sized rope – it will come undone.

TIMBER HITCH

An incredibly easy knot to tie. Very secure and very easy to undo. Used for dragging or securing objects to heavy logs.

WILD PLANT FOOD

There are very few areas in the world where plant life does not exist. Even in the most inhospitable places, you can normally find some type of vegetation growing.

EDIBLE PLANTS

Learn to recognise those plants which will be of most use to you and where to find them. At the same time, learn the poisonous ones, so you can avoid them. The study of plants (botany) can help you more easily identify which ones are useful.

WHAT PART TO EAT

Only certain parts of a plant will be edible. It might be the root, the stem, the flower, the leaf or the fruit. You need to learn what part of a plant is safe to eat and how it should be prepared.

WHAT PLANTS TO AVOID

Your sense of sight and smell will give you a good indication whether a plant is safe to eat. If it looks unhealthy and smells of peach or bitter almonds, it is best avoided. Hemlock (above) is a very smelly and poisonous plant. Anything that irritates your skin or mouth is best left well alone. Never, ever eat a plant you are unsure about. It may make you very sick or even kill you.

COMMON EDIBLE PLANTS

Here are some common edible plants you may find useful in a survival situation.

STINGING NETTLES
(*Urtica Dioica*)

Nettles can be eaten in spring and early summer as a food. For the best taste, pick the tops and young leaves from plants only a few centimetres high. Larger leaves are bitter. Once cooked, they taste like spinach and contain useful amounts of Vitamin A and C, iron and other essential minerals. Always wear gloves to avoid being stung.

DANDELION
(*Taraxacum Officinale*)

A very widespread plant, it flowers from February to November. The roots can be boiled as a vegetable or roasted to make coffee.

The leaves are rich in Vitamin A and young leaves can be eaten raw.

CATTAIL

(*Typha Latifolia*)
This is an amazing source of carbohydrate, especially in winter, when other plant growth has disappeared. You can make flour from the roots, weave with the leaves and the fine down found on the stems burns well on camp fires.

NUTS

There are several species of tree that provide an edible nut. This includes hazel, sweet chestnut, walnut, beech, pine and oak. Nuts supply us with proteins, carbohydrate and fat.

HAZEL
(Corylus Avellana)

Very common throughout Europe, most often as a shrub rather than a tree. Hazel produces nuts from late August to October, at the same time as the leaves begin to yellow. Hazel nuts contain 50% more protein, seven times more fat and five times more carbohydrate than hens' eggs !!

SWEET CHESTNUT
(*Castinea Sativa*)

Chestnut trees are a fairly common tree in Europe and North America. Be sure not to mix up with horse chestnut, whose nuts (conkers) are poisonous. Chestnuts are delicious when roasted.

OAK (*Quercus Robur*)

Common throughout the world, the oak produces the familiar acorns every year. They can be used as a coffee substitute or as a food. Be sure to soak or boil in several changes of water before you eat them otherwise they are very bitter.

PINE (*Pinus*)

Found in most temperate and northern climates. The pinecones contain seeds which are best eaten by being roasted. Very tasty!

FRUIT

There are many plants that produce fruit we can eat.

BLACKBERRIES

Almost everyone is familiar with picking blackberries during summer. Widespread and common in many countries, the fruit is incredibly tasty and also very easily identifiable. Wild fruit doesn't just taste nice; it is very good for you as well. It provides you with some essential vitamins, especially A and C, which you need in your diet.

WARNING!

The only sure way to eat a wild fruit safely is to positively identify it. If in doubt, it is better to leave well alone and concentrate on finding safer sources of food.

COMMONLY AVAILABLE WILD FRUIT INCLUDES

Bilberry	Vaccinium Myrttillus
Rose Hips	Rosa
Wild Raspberries	Rubus Idaeus
Haws (from Hawthorn trees)	Crataegus Monogyna
Wild strawberries	Fragaria Vesca

The best way to learn about wild foods is to read about a different wild food every week and how you should eat it. In a year you will have learned about 52 plants you can eat. Multiply that by several years and you will have a very impressive knowledge.

WILD MEDICINE

Until relatively recently, most medical treatment was based on using wild herbs and plants.

IN USE TODAY

Many of today's drugs and medicines come from plants and herbs. The medicines which are extracted from them can be used to stop bleeding, cure fevers, relieve aches and pains, stop diarrhoea, clean wounds, and so on. The Amazonian rainforest is often a source of new plant medicines.

COMMON PLANTS TO USE

Comfrey – One of the most remarkable plants for natural remedies, it can be used for aches, pains, bruises, colds and as a poultice. The root is the most commonly used part.

Elder – another remarkably useful plant. Pages and pages are devoted to it in herbal remedy books. It can be used to treat fevers and constipation, epilepsy and sore throats.

Thyme – the common herb is very useful in making an antiseptic solution. The leaves and flowers have boiling water poured over them. Once cooled it can be used.

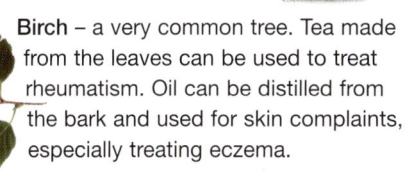

Birch – a very common tree. Tea made from the leaves can be used to treat rheumatism. Oil can be distilled from the bark and used for skin complaints, especially treating eczema.

Blackberry – the root can be used for treating diarrhoea. A small amount of root is crushed and boiled in water. The liquid is then drunk every hour or two.

HEALTH AND HYGIENE

It is very important to keep yourself as clean as possible when you are outside or in the wilderness. Here are some tips to help you achieve this

GENERAL HYGIENE

Try to wash daily, paying particular attention to your hands, face, feet and personal areas. By doing this you can try to avoid any fungal infections, such as athlete's foot. Always wash your hands after going to the toilet and before cooking.

RUBBISH

If you don't dispose of rubbish properly, you will attract all sorts of unwelcome visitors to you. These can include rats, flies and ants. Ants might not seem the most threatening of creatures but they tend to visit in the thousands and rampage about!

TEETH

Teeth should always be cleaned daily. If you don't have a toothbrush you can make one from a twig. Hazel is a particularly good wood for this. Strip off the bark, chew one end and then use to gently clean around teeth and gums.

POSITIVE MENTAL ATTITUDE

It is very important to keep your morale up. One of the best ways to do this is to keep busy. Set yourself lots of small tasks, rather than big ones. Success, no matter how small, makes you feel better.

BASIC MOUNTAIN SAFETY

It is very important that you make any trip into the mountains as safe as possible.

BASIC EQUIPMENT

You don't need to spend a lot of money to equip yourself for the hills. You need comfortable boots and socks, waterproofs, a map and compass, a hat, gloves, a rucksack, a jumper to put on when you stop and food and drink. You should also carry a whistle, a small first aid kit and an emergency bivvi bag.

WINTER CONDITIONS

If you go walking in the mountains in winter, you will need to carry a few extra items. This includes some additional warm clothing and spare gloves and hat.

NAVIGATION

The key skill to getting about in the mountains is navigation. If you can't use a map, you should not go off obvious tracks. When you can use a map and compass properly, your time in mountainous terrain is not only much more enjoyable, it is a great deal safer too.

TRIP PLAN

Accidents can, and will, happen in the mountains. Every year people have accidents or get lost in mountains. You should complete a trip plan and leave it with someone responsible. This is the best way for the emergency service to find you if something does go wrong.

Trip Plan

What to take:
Map
Compass
Hat
Gloves
Extra Jumpers
Torch
Whistle
First Aid Kit

Route Plan:

1) We will start at 9.00am from the Church of St Andrew and walk through Rushmere wood Warren Heath.

2) From the Fountain we will follow the river footpath through Farmer Jones' field to the O

3) We will eat lunch at about 1 Orwell Bridge.

4) We will walk back Warren Heath.

From the Fount
will set
for the night.

RECOGNISING ANIMAL TRACKS

It is very easy to find out what animals are in an area if you can identify their tracks and signs.

'PERFECT' TRACKS

It is rare to see perfect tracks so a good knowledge of tracking and signs will help you. Start by identifying easy tracks, such as in soft or muddy ground which is free of any plant growth. Sand dunes very early in the morning are also good. The best (and easiest) tracks to find are those in snow.

WHERE TO LOOK

The easiest place to start is an animal path. Most animal use the same path or paths to get to and from their home, feeding place and watering spot. You will find them along walls, banks and running through the undergrowth.

WHAT TO LOOK FOR

You are looking for clues that show you what animal made the tracks. Size, depth and width will tell you what animal made the print, the rough age of the animal (old or young) and in what direction it was going and how fast. If it is a definite, sharp track then it is fairly recent. The older the track, the more distorted it will be.

MAKING YOUR OWN TRACK CASTS

Its easy to make a plaster mould of any animal tracks you find.

You Will Need:
Plaster of Paris, 250 ml of water, a jug, a bowl and a spoon

1 First, mix together the plaster of Paris with water (approx 250 g of powder to 250 ml of water).

2 Gently pour the mixture into the animal track. Be careful not to spill any.

3 Leave them to dry. Do not touch them for at least five hours, even if they look dry. When the plaster is dry remove them from the track.

TECHNIQUES TO SHARPEN SENSES

Humans rely on five senses, with sight being the most important. You can develop three of your senses to help you survive. These are sight, hearing and smell.

SIGHT

Take time to look properly. We overlook much of what we see because we rush. Relax and take more time to look at things. Look thoroughly. Learn to sweep the ground with your eyes.

HEARING

The best way to hear more in any wood/forest is simple – listen more and make less noise. Walk slowly and quietly and keep any talking to a minimum. Stop often to listen. Animals run away from the noise you make.

SMELL

Your sense of smell will become more developed as you spend more time in the wild. After a relatively short space of time (7 days or so) you will start to smell like the environment around you. You may even start to smell things before you see them.

NATURAL NAVIGATION

There are millions and millions of stars in the night sky. We can use some of them to help us navigate.

POLARIS

In the northern hemisphere, Polaris, or the North Star, will accurately show you the direction of north. It is always within one or two degrees of North. There are several constellations that we can use to help us find the North Star.

THE PLOUGH

The two stars from the plough we are interested in are called Duble (x) and Merak (y). The two stars point beyond Dubble, almost exactly to the Pole star (z), about five times further away than the distance between them.

USING THE SUN

The sun is very useful as an aid to direction. It rises in the east and sets in the west. At midday in the northern hemisphere, the sun is always due south and at midday in the southern hemisphere it is due north.

SHADOW CLOCK

You can use shadows to accurately work out direction. Find a patch of clear ground and stick a straight pole, some about a metre long, into the ground. Mark with a twig where the tip of the shadow falls. Wait 15–20 minutes and mark where the tip of the shadow has moved to. The first mark is west, the second is east. By placing your left foot by the first mark and your right foot by the second, you will now be facing north.

MORSE CODE

Morse code is a simple signing system that allows you to communicate with others.

Full stop .-.-.-   Comma --..--   Query ..--..

A	.-	O	---	2	..---
B	-...	P	.--.	3	...--
C	-.-.	Q	--.-	4	....-
D	-..	R	.-.	5	.....
E	.	S	...	6	-....
F	..-.	T	-	7	--...
G	--.	U	..-	8	---..
H	....	V	...-	9	----.
I	..	W	.--		
J	.---	X	-..-		
K	-.-	Y	-.--		
L	.-..	Z	--..		
M	--	0	-----		
N	-.	1	.----		

Use the code torch provided with this kit to learn and practise the Morse Code.